P9-DGB-504

CROFTON MEADOWS ELEMENTARY
MEDIA CENTER

Guinea Pigs
and other Rodents

Bobbie Kalman & Reagan Miller

🜊 Crabtree Publishing Company

www.crabtreebooks.com

Created by Bobbie Kalman

Dedicated by Reagan Miller
For Allan Ivey, my dear friend, great love, and teammate for life's adventures

Editor-in-Chief
Bobbie Kalman

Writing team
Bobbie Kalman
Reagan Miller

Substantive editor
Kelley MacAulay

Editors
Molly Aloian
Robin Johnson
Kathryn Smithyman

Design
Katherine Kantor
Samantha Crabtree (cover)

Production coordinator
Heather Fitzpatrick

Photo research
Crystal Foxton

Consultant
Patricia Loesche, Ph.D., Animal Behavior Program, Department of Psychology, University of Washington

Special thanks to
Devan Cruickshanks

Illustrations
Barbara Bedell: pages 4 (porcupine and capybara), 5 (mouse, squirrel, and rat),
    9, 11 (all except beaver), 13, 14 (nuts), 15 (worm), 29, 30, 31 (bottom),
    32 (capybaras, incisors, jerboas, mice, porcupines, rats, and squirrels)
Antoinette "Cookie" Bortolon: page 14 (seeds and berries)
Katherine Kantor: page 15 (insect)
Jeannette McNaughton-Julich: pages 11 (beaver), 22, 23
Bonna Rouse: pages 4 (guinea pig), 5 (beaver), 7, 8, 14 (grass), 19, 32 (backbone,
    beavers, guinea pigs, and lungs)
Margaret Amy Salter: pages 5 (prairie dog), 17, 31 (top), 32 (babies and prairie dogs)

Photographs
©Maier, Robert/Animals Animals - Earth Scenes: page 17
Marc Crabtree: page 6
iStockphoto.com: pages 18, 20 (left), 21 (top), 24, 25 (top), 29 (top)
Bobbie Kalman: page 12 (top)
Photo Researchers Inc.: Gregory G. Dimijian: page 15 (bottom);
    Tom & Pat Leeson: page 16
Other images by Corel, Creatas, Digital Vision, Eye Wire Images, and Photodisc

---

Crabtree Publishing Company

www.crabtreebooks.com   1-800-387-7650

Copyright © **2006 CRABTREE PUBLISHING COMPANY**.
All rights reserved. No part of this publication may be reproduced, stored in a retrieval system or be transmitted in any form or by any means, electronic, mechanical, photocopying, recording, or otherwise, without the prior written permission of Crabtree Publishing Company. In Canada: We acknowledge the financial support of the Government of Canada through the Book Publishing Industry Development Program (BPIDP) for our publishing activities.

Cataloging-in-Publication Data
Kalman, Bobbie.
  Guinea pigs and other rodents / Bobbie Kalman & Reagan Miller.
    p. cm. -- (What kind of animal is it?)
  ISBN-13: 978-0-7787-2163-5 (rlb)
  ISBN-10: 0-7787-2163-9 (rlb)
  ISBN-13: 978-0-7787-2221-2 (pbk)
  ISBN-10: 0-7787-2221-X (pbk)
  1. Rodents--Juvenile literature. I. Miller, Reagan. II. Title. III. Series.
  QL737.R6K284 2005
  599.35--dc22   2005022999
                                                          LC

**Published in
the United States**

PMB16A
350 Fifth Ave.
Suite 3308
New York, NY
10118

**Published
in Canada**

616 Welland Ave.,
St. Catharines, Ontario
Canada
L2M 5V6

**Published in the
United Kingdom**

73 Lime Walk
Headington
Oxford
OX3 7AD
United Kingdom

**Published
in Australia**

386 Mt. Alexander Rd.,
Ascot Vale (Melbourne)
VIC 3032

Contents

What are rodents?   4

Rodents are mammals   6

Rodent bodies   8

Rodents in action!   10

Rodent habitats   12

Mealtime!   14

Baby rodents   16

Guinea pigs   18

Mice and rats   20

Handy homemakers   22

Buried treasures   24

Prickly porcupines   26

Crazy for capybaras!   28

Have we met?   29

Rodent detectives   30

Words to know and Index   32

What are rodents?

guinea pig

Rodents are animals. They live all over the world. There are two main groups of rodents. All rodents belong to one of these two groups. Which rodents do you know?

Porcupine-jawed rodents

One group of rodents is called porcupine-jawed rodents. Guinea pigs, porcupines, and capybaras are some of the rodents in this group.

porcupine

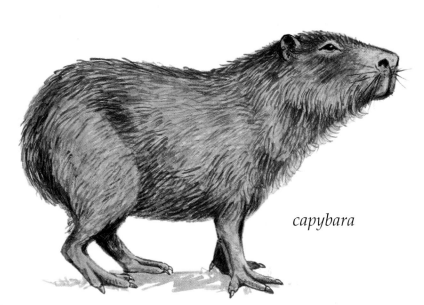

capybara

4

beaver

Squirrel-jawed rodents

The other group of rodents is called squirrel-jawed rodents. Prairie dogs, beavers, squirrels, rats, and mice are squirrel-jawed rodents.

mouse

squirrel

prairie dog

rat

Rodents are mammals

Rodents are **mammals**. Mammals are **warm-blooded** animals. The body temperatures of warm-blooded animals always stay about the same, even when the animals are in cold or hot places.

How are people and rodents the same? People and rodents are both mammals!

Breathing air

Like all mammals, rodents must breathe air to stay alive. Rodents use their **lungs** to breathe air. Lungs are body parts that take in air. Lungs also let out air. You have lungs inside your body, too!

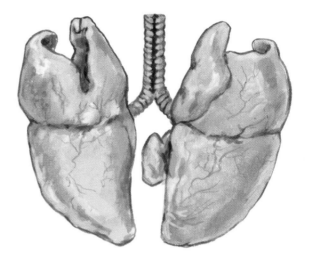

a guinea pig's lungs

These guinea pigs have lungs inside their bodies.

Make way for more on mammals!

Mammals are animals that
- have hair or fur on their bodies (See page 8.)
- have **backbones** inside their bodies (See page 8.)
- **nurse** when they are young (See page 16.)

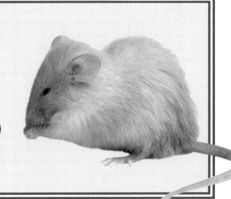

Rodent bodies

Most rodents have small bodies, but a few kinds of rodents have large bodies. All rodents have backbones inside their bodies. A backbone is a group of bones in the middle of an animal's back.

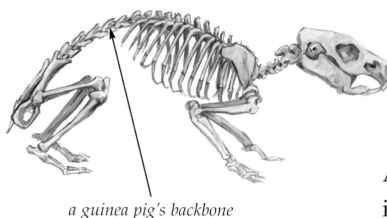

a guinea pig's backbone

Most rodents have small eyes. They cannot see objects that are far away.

Many rodents have small noses, but they can smell very well. They can smell food or other animals from far away.

Most rodents have fur or hair on their bodies. Fur helps them stay warm and dry.

Rodents have whiskers around their noses and above their eyes. As they move, rodents brush their whiskers against objects. Whiskers help rodents feel their way in the dark.

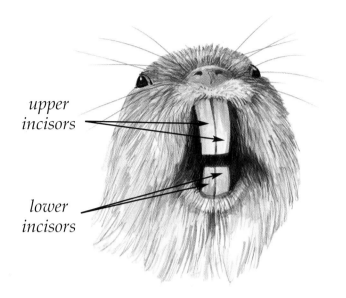

upper
incisors

lower
incisors

Rodents, such as this prairie dog, have strong teeth. Some rodents can even chew through steel wires!

Terrific teeth!

A rodent has sharp, pointed teeth at the front of its mouth. These teeth are called **incisors**. A rodent has two upper incisors and two lower incisors. A rodent's incisors never stop growing! A rodent chews on hard objects to keep its incisors short and sharp. It may chew on wood or nutshells.

This beaver is chewing on a tree to keep its teeth short and sharp. What do beavers build using trees? *Turn to page 23 to find out!*

Rodents in action!

Rodents move from place to place in many ways. Some rodents walk or run on land. Others swim in lakes, rivers, and ponds. Most rodents can climb trees. There are even rodents that can **glide!** To glide means to sail through the air. These pages show some of the different ways in which rodents move.

Porcupines walk slowly on land, but they climb trees quickly.

Flying squirrels live in trees. They move from tree to tree by gliding through the air.

Jerboas use their long back legs to jump quickly across grassy fields.

Squirrels are the fastest rodents. They run quickly on land and in trees.

Beavers are good swimmers. They use their tails to steer their bodies in water.

11

Rodent habitats

Some prairie dogs live in deserts.

Rodents live in different **habitats** all over the world. A habitat is the natural place where an animal lives. Many rodents live in habitats such as grassy fields and forests. Other rodents live on mountains or in **deserts**. Deserts are hot habitats that receive very little rain.

*Muskrats live in **wetlands**. Wetlands are areas of land, such as marshes, that are wet for at least part of the year.*

Groundhogs are also called woodchucks. They chew on wood found in the forests and fields where they live.

Do not disturb!

Many rodents live in places that have long, cold winters. Some rodents that live in these places **hibernate**. To hibernate means to sleep through winter. Rodents such as groundhogs and some squirrels hibernate in winter. The dormouse, shown left, may hibernate for as long as seven months each year!

Mealtime!

seeds

grass

Different rodents eat different foods. Most rodents are **herbivores**. Herbivores are animals that eat mainly plants. Many rodents that are herbivores eat seeds, berries, grass, nuts, and flowers.

berries

nuts

This groundhog is a herbivore. It is eating a flower.

14

Different diets

Many rodents are **omnivores**. Omnivores are animals that eat both plants and animals. A hamster is an omnivore. It eats seeds and grass. It also eats worms and insects.

hamster

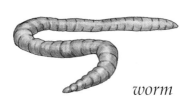
worm

insect

This harvest mouse is eating a butterfly. It also eats grass and seeds. It is an omnivore.

Baby rodents

Baby rodents are **born**. Animals that are born are not inside eggs when they come out of the bodies of their mothers. Rodent mothers make milk inside their bodies. Baby rodents nurse. To nurse means to drink mother's milk.

*Most baby rodents are born in **litters**. Litters are groups of babies. The baby beavers shown above are nursing. Their mother is also enjoying a snack! She is eating a piece of wood.*

Mom knows best!

Rodent mothers take good care of their babies. They teach their babies how to find food and how to stay safe. The babies learn by watching their mothers. When the rodents are a few months old, they are ready to leave their mothers and live on their own.

A baby guinea pig, shown above, is getting a ride on its mother's back! Some rodent mothers use their teeth to move their babies gently from place to place.

Guinea pigs

Many people keep guinea pigs as pets. At one time, all guinea pigs were **wild animals**. Wild animals are not cared for by people. Many wild guinea pigs still live in South America. They live in grassy fields and on rocky mountains.

*Wild guinea pigs live together in small groups. Each group has between five and ten guinea pigs. Guinea pig groups live in underground homes called **burrows**.*

Gabbing guinea pigs

Guinea pigs send messages to one another by making different sounds. Guinea pigs make high, squeaking sounds to warn other guinea pigs of danger. They make chirping sounds to tell other guinea pigs that food is nearby. Guinea pigs also send messages to one another using their bodies. For example, guinea pigs greet each other by touching noses.

This guinea pig has opened its mouth to show its sharp teeth. This action means the guinea pig is angry.

Guinea pigs do not "oink" like pigs!

Mice and rats are rodents that can live almost anywhere! They may live in dry deserts or near wetlands. Mice and rats often live close to people in houses, barns, and other buildings. Living near people helps these rodents find food. Mice and rats often eat leftover food that people have thrown away.

Mice and rats can stand on their back legs. Standing on their back legs helps these small rodents reach food. This rat has stopped to smell the flowers!

There is a mouse in the house! Mice and rats can squeeze their bodies through small openings. This wood rat has come through a small hole in a log cabin.

A late-night bite!

Many animals, such as snakes and birds, eat mice and rats. To avoid these animals, mice and rats often hide during the day. They come out at night to search for food. It is difficult for many other animals to see mice and rats in the dark. Animals that are mainly active at night are called **nocturnal** animals.

This snake is eating a mouse.

Handy homemakers

The homes prairie dogs and beavers make are different from the homes made by most other rodents. Read on to learn more about these rodents and their homes.

Out on the town

Prairie dogs live in groups called **families**. Prairie dog families dig burrows. Each family's burrow is connected to the burrows of other families. A large group of burrows is called a **town**. Some prairie dog towns are home to thousands of prairie dogs!

Each burrow has rooms for sleeping and eating.

Large lodges

Beaver families also build large homes! They build homes called **lodges** in deep, slow-moving waters. Beavers use their sharp teeth to cut down trees. They build their lodges using sticks and branches from the trees.

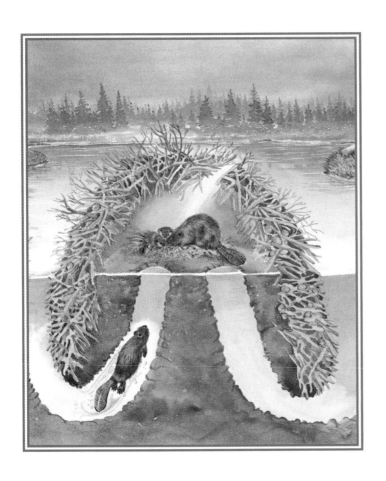

A beaver lodge has one big room. The room has places for the beavers to rest, store food, and care for their babies.

Do-it-yourself dams

Beavers sometimes build their lodges in **streams**. Streams are fast-moving waters. Fast-moving waters could wash away a beaver's lodge! Before building a lodge, beavers first build a **dam** in the stream. A dam is a wall of logs that slows down the water.

Buried treasures

Most squirrels and chipmunks live in places that have cold winters. It is hard for them to find food in winter. They gather food in autumn and save it for winter. Squirrels and chipmunks store some of the gathered food inside their homes. They bury the rest of the food in the ground. When squirrels and chipmunks get hungry, they dig up the buried food.

This chipmunk has stored some food in its home inside a log.

That is a mouthful!

Chipmunks and some squirrels have **pouches** inside their mouths. Pouches are small pockets. Chipmunks and squirrels stuff their pouches with food. They bring the food back to their homes.

This squirrel is filling its pouches with nuts and seeds.

Trees, please!

Did you know that some squirrels and chipmunks plant trees? Squirrels and chipmunks often do not eat all their stored food. They leave some nuts and seeds buried in the ground. Many of the nuts and seeds grow into trees!

Prickly porcupines

A porcupine's body is covered with sharp hairs. These hairs are called **quills**. Quills help keep a porcupine safe from other animals. When an animal bites a porcupine, the quills break off inside the animal's mouth. The animal then lets go of the porcupine, and the porcupine can escape.

A baby porcupine stays with its mother for about six months. The young porcupine then leaves its mother to find food on its own. This young porcupine is looking for leaves and flowers to eat.

Porcupines live in forests, deserts, and grassy fields. Many porcupines eat the bark, leaves, and berries that they find on trees.

Crazy for capybaras!

Capybaras are the largest rodents in the world! Capybaras live in South America. The weather in South America is always warm. Capybaras swim in lakes and rivers to keep their bodies cool. They are excellent swimmers!

It is hard to spot a capybara while it is swimming. The capybara's ears, eyes, and nose are the only parts of its body that you can see above the water.

 # Have we met?

There are thousands of kinds of rodents! This page shows some rodents that you may not have seen before.

Degus are found in South America. Large groups of degus live together in underground burrows.

Hoary marmots live in mountains in western North America. They are also known as "whistlers." Hoary marmots make loud, high sounds when they are scared.

Chinchillas live high in the mountains of South America. Mountain habitats are often windy and cold. Chinchillas have long fur that keeps them warm.

Rodent detectives

Rodents live all over the world. There are probably rodents living near your home! The next time you walk through a park, a field, or a forest, look for the clues shown on these pages to find out if rodents live nearby.

Going nuts!

If you find piles of nutshells and seed shells, it could mean that squirrels or chipmunks live in the area.

On the right track

Be sure to keep your eyes open for tracks that belong to rodents! The tracks will be easiest to see in mud or snow.

Who lives in here?

Be on the lookout for burrows in the ground. Burrows with small holes may belong to small rodents such as chipmunks or squirrels. Burrows with large holes may belong to groundhogs or prairie dogs.

Leaving their mark

If you see trees with bite marks on them or with pieces of bark missing, beavers could live nearby. You may also see tree stumps where beavers have chewed down trees.

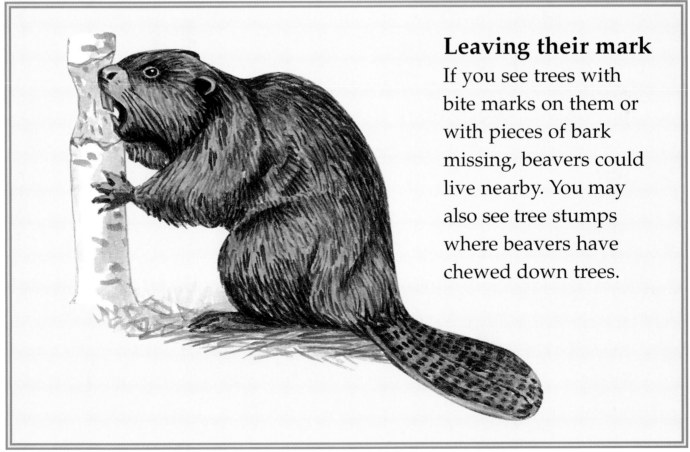

Words to know and Index

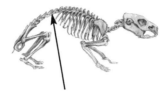

backbones
pages 7, 8

babies
pages 16-17, 23, 26
(nursing)
pages 7, 16

beavers
pages 5, 9, 11,
16, 22, 23, 31

capybaras
pages 4, 28

guinea pigs
pages 4, 7, 8,
17, 18-19

hamsters
page 15

**incisors
(teeth)**
pages 9, 17,
19, 23

jerboas
page 11

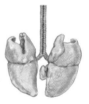

lungs
page 7

mice
pages 5, 13,
15, 20-21

porcupines
pages 4, 10,
26-27

prairie dogs
pages 5, 9,
12, 22, 31

rats
pages 5, 20-21

squirrels
pages 5, 11, 13,
24-25, 30, 31

Other index words

fur 7, 8, 29
habitats 12, 29
herbivores 14
hibernation 13
omnivores 15
warm blood 6

1 2 3 4 5 6 7 8 9 0   Printed in the U.S.A.   4 3 2 1 0 9 8 7 6 5